Your Own Living Blueprint

Your living blueprint is individual to your family. It is alive and may be constantly changing. Living blueprint is a method to look at the events, experiences, and people that develop your current life. It determines how you express your feelings, experience traditions, and pattern life. Why are some areas of your life difficult and confusing? How do these limits work towards developing a barrier in you achieving the parenting imprint for your child? How will the awareness of your limitations assist you in the development of providing tools that will support your child's mastery of new task? The question is, are you currently living at large or are you fully living your parenting blueprint.

What are your living childhood blueprints? What early imprints guide your communication style and social interaction level of comfort with self? What old grudges, past regrets, etc. sit at the dinner table with you, ride to work with you, or stop you from going forward towards your dreams. I often am questioned why ones childhood would impact their adult life behavior. When shopping for grocery how does what you have previously purchased influence what you chose. If what you currently have is rotten at home do you eat, or replace? If you discover a product did not agree with you and results in illness or discomfort do you continue to consume it or try something else? Your parenting blueprint is designed by you and your child. It is focused on addressing your child's individual personality. Your living blueprint is alive and always changing. It is also influencing your parenting relationship.

Make Your Mission Statement

What are your family's beliefs, goals, and expectations of members involved?

What are each parent's values and path of achievement?

Do you agree with united process?

Write a family mission statement. If you are co-parenting, are your statements in alignment with each other's?

Are you experiencing the parenting blueprint (the way you envisioned the parenting direction of your child)? If not, how would you like it to change?

How are you communicating your mission statement in your parenting style?

The Baby Sleeps Through the Night

As my husband remembers and has said several times, our children slept through the night at four months of age. To his surprise, I informed him, "No, *you* slept through the night. The baby was up." If you are a co-parent that is not informed of the struggles your child, tween, or teen is experiencing your interpretation of the co-parenting is different from the parent who is most informed. Strong, clear communication is a benefit in parenting it allows for a dual or multiple understanding of the child's behavior, activities and struggles.

Introspective Questions

List the moments you have been in the company of others and your co-parent describe a situation that you were unaware of concerning your child.

How could that have been handled differently?

The Phone is Off the Hook.

During a conversation with my husband when my son was a toddler, my husband stated the phone is off the hook. My son was focused on our words with stealth-like stillness. Communication includes the messages you are not trying to send. Children are always listening, but it is impossible to monitor every moment of every interaction. It is good to keep in mind that what children hear from parents may result in a longstanding point of view in relation to a person, issue, self-motivation, etc.

Introspective Questions

What conversations did you overhear your parents, adults, or older siblings saying when you were a child, tween, or teen?

How did overhearing that conversations change your view on that subject.

Examples of discussions to be mindful of include but are not limited to the following:

- Daily frustrations- age appropriate.
- Recently learned incidents.
- Loss of love ones, tragedies that may be over whelming to a child.
- Parents or caretakers using negative name calling.
- Details of feeling overwhelmed (especially concerning having children)
- Threats of parent or caretaker leaving the relationship child, tween or teen may view themselves as the reason for parent or caretaker leaving.
- Questions of infidelity.
- Strong disagreements occurring in child's room.

What's the Plan?

Supportive parenting allows for strategic involvement that supports the parent's mission statement while infusing the individual traits that lead you to choose these individuals as your supportive parent network. Childhood can have a significant influence on the foundation of your mind your network is part of building that foundation.

Introspective Questions

What new dynamic has been experienced by your child in the last year?

List your selected supportive childcare network individuals.

Plan a meeting a simple as a conversation on the phone or in person and discuss with the individual(s) chosen for your parent support network.

What events would trigger the requirement of this needed additional support?

Sorry, I Didn't Understand What You Were Saying.

Is your communication an intervention that seamlessly guides your child toward your parenting blueprint or is your communication a direct interference? Do you focus on what would result in your child's success or are your actions an attempt to re-parent your inner child?

Clear communication sounds easy but often parenting includes all the influences of each parent. Family meeting are a good time not only to get together but to discuss with children (of course only when age appropriate you decide). The senior team (parents) should meet separately without children present prior to the family meeting. This allows each parent's views, disagreements and strategies to be communicated in a child free environment. It allows for the development of a united parent approach, roles and expectations.

The family meeting with children should also be a time to reflect on the progress made by children to achieve goals big and small. It can also offer a support for unsuccessful attempts to achieve goals and guidance toward the next step. This can be a great opportunity to share effective methods to use family tools, community resources, or family activities that will support the achievement of the family member's desired goal.

List your goals as parents for the next year.

1)

2)

3)

4)

What resources, training,and activities will assist you in the achievement of your goals as a parent?

A Gift Box

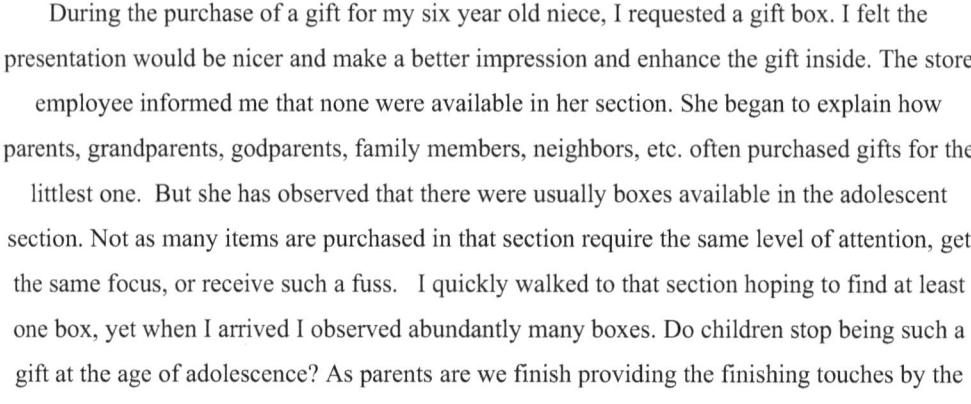

During the purchase of a gift for my six year old niece, I requested a gift box. I felt the presentation would be nicer and make a better impression and enhance the gift inside. The store employee informed me that none were available in her section. She began to explain how parents, grandparents, godparents, family members, neighbors, etc. often purchased gifts for the littlest one. But she has observed that there were usually boxes available in the adolescent section. Not as many items are purchased in that section require the same level of attention, get the same focus, or receive such a fuss. I quickly walked to that section hoping to find at least one box, yet when I arrived I observed abundantly many boxes. Do children stop being such a gift at the age of adolescence? As parents are we finish providing the finishing touches by the teen years. Most of all are they waiting for just a little giftwrap.

Introspective Questions

Did you experience an age where you no longer felt like a gift? When did your childhood change direction?

Did you feel lost?

Remember no matter if infant, toddler, child, tween or teen be aware of what stage of the gift is your child.

Parent Company

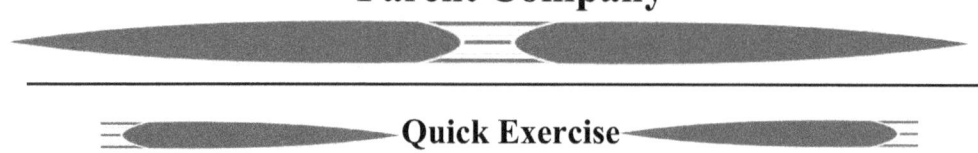

If being a parent was a business, what is your businesses work ethic?

Do you work extra hours? Do you network? How well do you know your product (your child/children)? How well do you know the products demographics (the children in your child's class at the playground, images they exposed to, other influence,etc.)

Are these skills used in your obtaining services for daycare, education, doctor's visit, etc.? For instance, do you research the potential service, have you already established expectations, and are you an active member the process?

Which parent attends which activity?

Why are you choosing this approach?

How do you use technology to stay informed and achieve the best supportive outcome?

Note to Child

I told my daughter that the day she was born I had to be told by the doctor to get off the phone because the baby was coming. She thinks that is the funniest story she's ever heard and she still is on the phone today. I don't know where she gets that from. The day of your child's birth is their first living blueprint. The day your child was born, adopted, or included in your life is a great way to express your joy of that day.

Quick Exercise

Talk with your child, tween or teen about your life at their current age.

Discuss your day from the moment you woke up. Describe your room, what was in it, what you ate for breakfast, and your transition to school.

What where your challenges and limitation.

You decide what is age-appropriate and how much you want to share. Allow questions, of course, at your comfort level.

Share your childhood fears, dreams, challenges, social relationships struggles and successes.

This allows a model for exchange of daily experiences. This is a time to say how your experience can assist your child in their journey.

Watch out

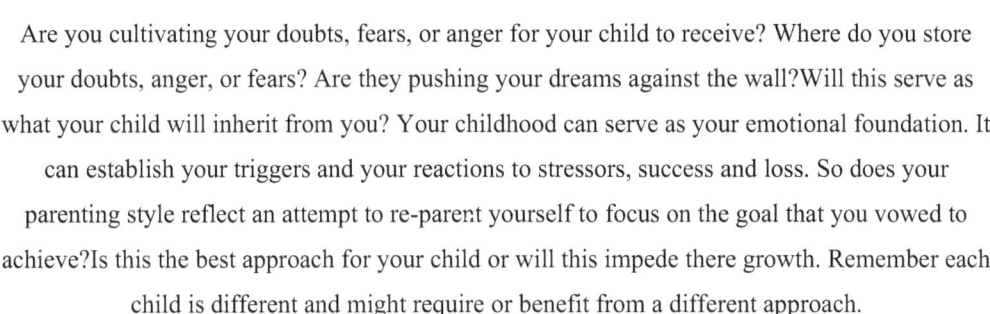

Are you cultivating your doubts, fears, or anger for your child to receive? Where do you store your doubts, anger, or fears? Are they pushing your dreams against the wall?Will this serve as what your child will inherit from you? Your childhood can serve as your emotional foundation. It can establish your triggers and your reactions to stressors, success and loss. So does your parenting style reflect an attempt to re-parent yourself to focus on the goal that you vowed to achieve?Is this the best approach for your child or will this impede there growth. Remember each child is different and might require or benefit from a different approach.

Introspective Questions

Who are the key holders of your fears doubts and anger?

What are your emotional triggers?

Some examples are:

- Bullies
- Wanting to fit in
- Moving to new house, job, school, etc.
- Not being selected
- Dating
- Divorce
- Violence
- Commitment
- Rejection
- Fear of situation
- Childhood Reunions

List your known triggers of your child's behavior.

1)

2)

3)

4)

5)

6)

When you respond to them is it to assist them in emotional support or isyour responses guided by your feelings about the trigger?

Is the response in the target of your child's long-term success?

How does it feel to see your response in writing?

Now What?

Life often incudes change. Moving to new neighborhood, change in school location, adjustments in income, family illness, and sudden loss of loved ones can all can be devastating to those involved. These events may become overwhelming and deplete the emotional energy of parents, but the demand of daily child care continues to remain. How do you prepare your child for a pending change or transition? A crisis or sudden change can result in an impulsive childcare plan. Advance care plan provides support systems that can be communicated with any adult the parent determines would benefit from such information.

A child also experiences independent struggles, attempts to master a skill, and feeling the energy of family and environmental emotional stressors. Changes in behaviors or methods of communication, such as verbal child becoming withdrawn, should be explored with your child. Has there been a change in his/her daily interacting with the world? Check for a new dynamic in peer groups, new playmates, upcoming socialization events, or new family stressor.

Introspective Questions

How many family stressors in the last 2 years have you experienced?

How were the stressors handled?

Have a Seat

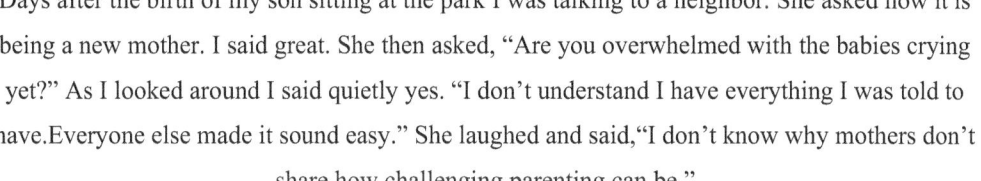

Days after the birth of my son sitting at the park I was talking to a neighbor. She asked how it is being a new mother. I said great. She then asked, "Are you overwhelmed with the babies crying yet?" As I looked around I said quietly yes. "I don't understand I have everything I was told to have.Everyone else made it sound easy." She laughed and said,"I don't know why mothers don't share how challenging parenting can be."

This is the beginning of my sharing my experiences of parenthood. Live your living parenting blueprint.

www.ingramcontent.com/pod-product-compliance
Lightning Source LLC
Chambersburg PA
CBHW070942290526
45795CB00003B/1117